MATH WITH
CONNECTING
PEOPLE

MATH WITH
CONNECTING
PEOPLE

ROSAMOND WELCHMAN-TISCHLER

Written by: Rosamond Welchman-Tischler
Edited by: Judith Adams
Illustrated by: Mena Dolobowsky
Interior design by: Leslie Bauman and Molly Heron
Line art by: Kay Wanous
Cover design by: Dave Metzger

© 1995, 2001 Learning Resources, Inc., Vernon Hills, Illinois (U.S.A.)
            Learning Resources Ltd., King's Lynn, Norfolk (U.K.)

ISBN: 1-56911-023-9

Printed in U.S.A.

TABLE OF CONTENTS

INTRODUCTION

MEETING THE CONNECTING PEOPLE

The Connecting People have an irresistible appeal to young and old. A child presented with a set of Connecting People will immediately get involved with the pieces, arranging the People, and building stories around them. A set of little People is colorful and friendly, yet has an interesting structure that suggests a wide range of uses for teaching mathematics.

The Connecting People come in four colors, red, green, blue, and yellow. They also come in three sizes and in male and female versions. In a complete set of 96 People there are exactly four of each possible combination of these attributes. The Connecting People can stand up, and their hands have pegs and holes so that they can be snapped together.

If you have not had an opportunity to handle the Connecting People, you should do so now. Put yourself in the position of a child exploring them for the first time. What do you notice about them? What sorts of arrangements can you make with them? How could you use them?

The experience chart below summarizes what some first graders noticed about the People after a few days of free exploration with them.

Teacher:	What can you do with Connecting People?
Anna:	You can make patterns.
Elizabeth:	You can put them in size order.
Danny:	You can make families.
Ben:	You can make up stories.
Matthew:	They can hold hands.
Ran-de:	You can count them.
Jonathan:	You can make a spiral with them.
Angelica:	They can balance.
Justin:	You can put them in a straight line.
Ari:	You can make a family tree.
Francesca:	You can make a school of kids.
Krista:	You can make a girl-boy pattern.
Ghenet:	You can make them fall down like dominoes.
Anna:	They can hold hands in a curve.
Samantha:	People can hold hands upside down with people standing right-side up.
Simon:	You can organize them by color and size.
Abigail:	You can play a game like tic-tac-toe. You could win by getting three boys or three girls or three of the same color or size in a row.

PURPOSE OF THIS BOOK

The purpose of this book is to support classroom use of the Connecting People in grades K to 3 to teach mathematics in ways consistent with the vision of the

Curriculum Standards proposed by the National Council of Teachers of Mathematics. These Standards envision four generic themes underlying the study of mathematics—problem solving, reasoning, communication, and mathematical connections. This book is designed to promote these themes, providing teachers with 35 activity pages for children, arranged in clusters around major mathematical ideas. The 35 activities have the following features:

- Each activity requires children to be problem solvers. In general there is no one right answer. The activities require communication (spoken or written) of strategies and ways of thinking. The activities are suitable for a range of abilities, since different levels of thinking can be brought to the same challenge.
- The activity pages are designed to be used interactively, always requiring manipulation of Connecting People. Sometimes the pages involve formats in which People are to be placed on the page.
- The activity pages are not intended as worksheets. Since most of the activities are open-ended, children can do them over and over again and benefit from each experience. Sometimes there are suggestions for recording systems that children can copy. Often, children are encouraged to design their own recording systems rather than just filling in blanks in a prescribed format.
- Since the activities are intended for young children who may not yet be reading fluently, the pages rely on both words and pictures to communicate. The language is such that pages might be read by some first and most second graders. As needed, you will read the text to or along with children, and pictures or diagrams serve to remind them of these oral directions.

ORGANIZATION OF THIS BOOK

The activities are organized into clusters. A section for teachers at the beginning of each cluster offers an overview and suggests ways to develop, extend, and vary the activities to suit different grade levels, types of classroom organization, and materials.

The first cluster, *Introducing Connecting People*, provides a context for developing and sharing language related to the materials. These activities should be done first. The other clusters, however, can be approached by children in any order. Activities within a cluster sometimes build skills and are to be done in sequence. At other times they can be done in any order. You be the judge.

The six other clusters are as follows:

- *Making Patterns with Connecting People* builds on the way in which the People can be joined hand-to-hand and on children's natural tendency to form some sort of pattern in such a string.
- *Telling People Stories* uses some of the natural ways in which children talk about the People to provide contexts for mathematical concepts.

- *Classifying Connecting People* poses problems using various methods of classification, including loops, or Venn diagrams.
- *Using an Attribute Set of Connecting People* uses the structure of a special set of the People that includes just one of each type of person.
- *Measuring with Connecting People* leads children to use the People both as units of measure and as objects to be measured.
- *Collecting Data about Connecting People* involves skills of estimation, performing experiments, tallying, and displaying results.

Connecting People are especially suitable for teaching this wide range of mathematical topics because they provide a bridge between children's real experiences with people in their lives and more abstract and/or symbolic mathematical experiences. It is important, however, to give children varied physical experiences using different manipulatives that have the same underlying characteristics so that they see the commonalties and build abstractions. Activities done here with Connecting People can also be done with other materials. In fact, the organization of the book by the varied characteristics of the material makes it easy to imagine how each cluster could be done with other materials as well.

GENERAL CLASSROOM HINTS

Getting started   Allow children to explore the Connecting People freely before you begin more structured activities. Children will probably discover many of the mathematical themes developed in the activities in this book. When they have come across an idea themselves, they will have a sense of ownership and will be readier to investigate the idea in depth.

Free exploration also gives you the chance to listen for children's language that relates to mathematical ideas behind the People. Language of color and size may emerge easily, but children may need to clarify vocabulary related to gender. Children may use the terms "boy" and "girl" or "mother" and "father," which are age related. The general terms "male" and "female" are preferable, with "gender" as a term to describe this attribute. (Children may need to be introduced to the term "gender.") They might also refer to the differences in another way—"pants" or "skirts"—and use "clothing" as the general term.

It is difficult to say just how much time children need for free exploration. Allow children to continue as long as new ideas keep emerging or as long as they remain interested. From time to time, encourage children to share their observations, perhaps by adding to an experience chart such as the one on page 7.

Importance of communication   In all cases your interaction with children as they work is vital. The activities are built around specific mathematical ideas that emerge as children work with the Connecting People in specific ways. At the same time, the nature of Connecting People invites children to explore on their own, and valuable learning inevitably takes place under these circumstances, also. The challenge for you is to encourage children's exploration and experimentation with the Connecting People and also to make sure children understand how to do a particular activity. The only way to do this is to be alert to the actions and words of each individual child. Go over the instructions together. When you see that a child has not understood how an activity is to be carried out, find a way to guide the child back without interrupting other valuable learning or stifling the child's curiosity and natural tendency to explore and test his or her own ideas.

Talk with children as they work and help them become comfortable with paying attention to their own reasoning processes and using language to describe them. Above all, appreciate and nurture different learning styles and different ways of problem solving.

Children at all levels should be encouraged to communicate their thinking about the activities. This communication can be verbal (oral or written) or visual. You may have young children talk about their observations, while you write them on an experience chart like the one shown earlier. Several activity pages have a question to be talked about at the bottom. The commentary for teachers points out some ideas that you might listen for or encourage children to develop and share with others. Always encourage children to talk or write about their experiences according to their skill and developmental levels.

Recording of results in some way is very important, both for children who are learning about means of recording experiences and for you as you try to keep track of individual children's work in a busy classroom. Rubber stamps with images of the Connecting People are available for purchase. Children can use these and then color in the images to record their work or to design puzzles and challenges for other children. You can also make many copies of the drawings on pages 76 and 77 for children to cut, paste, and color. Children can also draw People and in so doing will probably develop some sort of symbolism to be sure that attributes of size or color are communicated easily and clearly.

Using Connecting People in different classroom structures   Connecting People can be used in many different classroom contexts. In their initial free exploration with the materials, children will probably work in small groups or individually (unless you have a large supply of the materials). Later on you may want to introduce the activities to the whole class.

One example of an activity in which a whole class can participate, using only one set of Connecting People, is described in the teacher's introduction for the cluster *Collecting Data about Connecting People*. In this activity each child selects just one of the Connecting People and the whole class develops ways to describe its selections by making a graph—first placing actual People on a grid and then coloring in spaces to correspond to these placements.

A number of the activities specify that they should be done with a partner or in a small group. Some of these are games that require a certain number of players, either to increase the excitement or to assume different roles. Activities that do not state the need for partners or larger groups can be done by individual children. In general it is desirable for children to work together because they will develop their abilities to share both materials and ideas, and they will learn from one another. You should make sure, however, that individual children are not inhibited by their more verbal or aggressive peers. Some activities in this book are thought-provoking puzzles in which some children should not be rushed by other children who sees a solution more quickly than they do. In your classroom you will doubtless find various ways to use the Connecting People—whole class, small group, and individual.

Developing a classroom file of activities   Since the activity pages can be used many times even by an individual student, you might find it useful to copy each one onto cardstock, and laminate them for repeated use. You can also put them in plastic covers in a looseleaf binder.

Many activities in this book provide a model for further similar activities that children can design themselves. (For examples see *Holding Hands, Take Ten, Guess the Labels* and *Footprint Puzzles*.) As children work on these activities, keep a supply of large file cards or sheets of paper available. Children's work can be laminated or put in a protective sleeve for a durable supply of further challenges. You can quickly develop a box of file cards or a loose leaf binder with student-generated problems, which can be used by other children in the class.

Storing the Connecting People   For some activities you can keep a full set of Connecting People in a box. Keeping this box near a block corner will encourage children to incorporate the People into block building.

Some activities—especially those in Cluster 5, *Using an Attribute Set of Connecting People*—call for a package containing a special set of 24 People. This attribute set consists of exactly one of each type of person; that is, of each combination of gender, color, and size. There are four attribute sets in each full set. You might keep each attribute set in a heavy duty plastic bag that can be thumbtacked to a bulletin board. Periodically you can challenge children to straighten out the bags, making sure that no one is missing and that these bags have no duplicates.

RESOURCES AT THE END OF THE BOOK

The end of the book contains pages with images that may be useful when presenting the activities to children. There are pictures and symbols to use when you prepare some materials required by the activities (for example, dice or spinners) and other materials that you might design. There are also formats for graphs which you may or may not want to use depending on your children's abilities and experience with designing their own ways to record.

1 INTRODUCING CONNECTING PEOPLE

The following five activities enable children to develop and use language as they describe the attributes of the Connecting People—color, size, and gender—and the mathematical processes they engage in—for example, patterning and sorting. These activities should build on prior free exploration, without explicit direction from you. Children discover many properties of the Connecting People on their own. Encourage them to share their experiences and record their observations on an experience chart. Given sufficient time, your students will probably come up with a wide range of discoveries about sorting, patterns, and numerical relationships.

All the activities in this section can be done with a 24-piece attribute set, but it doesn't matter if there are a few pieces more or less.

ARRANGING PEOPLE   PAGE 16

Materials: Connecting People

Children naturally look for ways to impose structure on their surroundings. Here children arrange Connecting People in some way so that when children close their eyes while other children move a piece, they can tell what change was made.

At first children might seem to rely only on memory in this activity. With practice, they discover more powerful ways to think with the Connecting People. They learn to arrange People in a spatial structure or in groups according to number, color, or gender and size. Identifying a piece that is moved is more difficult if children select only a random handful of Connecting People. It is easier if they select pieces that fit into a pattern, for example, all red People of different sizes and gender, repeating for another color, and so on. Children can even use all 24 pieces of the attribute set in an array. If you leave the choice of pieces open to children and allow them to share their experiences over many trials, they will discover for themselves the advantages of making deliberate choices.

WHO GOES IN THE HOUSE?   PAGE 17

Materials: Connecting People

Children guess the rule for sorting by attribute and then create and guess each other's sorting rules.

Children tend to sort the People based on one attribute without prompting. This activity helps children to progress from sorting by one attribute, for example, color, to sorting by another (gender or size) or by two attributes at once (color and size). If children persist in sorting by just one attribute after a number of trials, you may need to model other ways of sorting.

GROUPS OF PEOPLE   PAGE 18

Materials: Connecting People

During free exploration children often use Connecting People to represent their families or other people they know. (Children may give the People names and have them talk like people they know.) In *Groups of People,* this association is made explicit. Working in pairs, children compare two groups of People and then make their own groups of People to compare.

You may choose to describe this activity in terms of "families" instead of "groups." Since this may touch on sensitive issues for some children, you might discuss what a family consists of. Whether or not you suggest this terminology, children may refer to the Connecting People as family members anyway.

To prepare, introduce children to the practice of naming similarities and differences in classroom contexts that appeal to children, such as comparing two favorite books, two classroom pets, or two pictures. This encourages children to use their growing vocabulary and allows you to assess their abilities to perceive similarities and differences.

Follow up with a whole-class survey of families. Have each child make his or her family with the People and then arrange the results on a graph. An obvious way to sort families is by the number of people in each, but children might also sort by number of children. If you do not have enough Connecting People for a physical representation, have children draw them. Be sure that all children draw on the same size paper, small enough to fit on a large wall chart.

Number of people in our families

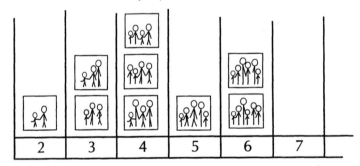

DICE GAME   PAGE 19

Materials: Connecting People; one standard die; three teacher-made dice (see templates on page 76)

Students collect Connecting People according to attributes that are determined by rolling dice.

One of the dice is standard, with numbers from 1 to 6. Children choose the other die from among three special dice with the attributes of the Connecting People—color, size, and gender. The color die can repeat two of the four colors or, if you wish, you can make it with the four colors and one happy face (indicating that any color can be taken) and one sad face (indicating that no pieces can be taken).

Children may first play this as a game of pure chance. After they play the game several times, however, and share their thinking, they realize that they can increase their chances of winning through the choice of dice. For example, because there are only two genders, choosing the gender die early in the game can yield up to six pieces. But if all the females have been taken, choosing the gender die is risky. The strategies children learn in this game can lay an intuitive foundation for the later study of probability.

SPINNER GAME   PAGE 20

Materials: Connecting People; one teacher-made die with numbers from 1 to 3; three spinners (see templates on page 78 for use with transparent spinners or use a pencil and paper clip with spinner faces on student page 20)

This game extends the previous one. Children roll a special number die to determine how many of three spinners—color, gender, or size—to use. They then take all the remaining People that satisfy the combination of attributes on the spinners.

The choice of spinner can have more of an effect on this game than the choice of die in the *Dice Game.* Suppose that on a first turn, a player rolls a "1." If that player then selects the gender spinner, he or she will be guaranteed half of the People. The size spinner, however, gives the player only a third of the People, and the color spinner a quarter of the People. At later points in the game, though, it might make sense to take either the color or size spinner if a "1" is not rolled (for example, if all of one gender have been taken, but there are still some of each color or size).

Children should play this game several times and share their experiences and discoveries each time. Ask children how and why they might want to change the rules to make the game more enjoyable.

ARRANGING PEOPLE

Work with a partner.

1. Take some People and arrange them in a pattern you can remember.

2. Close your eyes while your partner moves one of the People.

3. Open your eyes. Which person was moved?

Change roles. Try this many times.

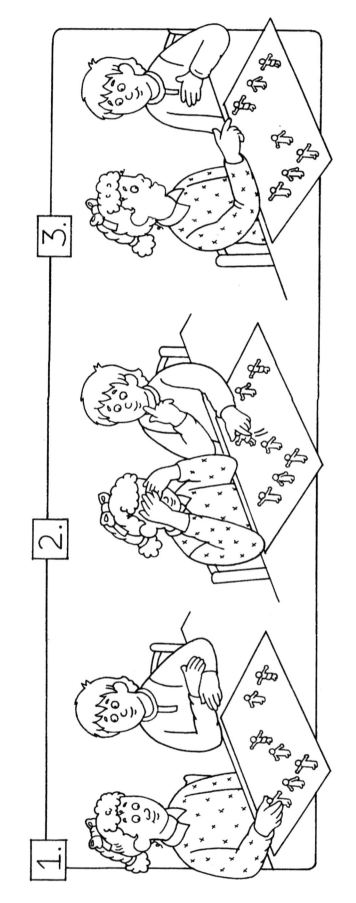

Talk with your partner about how you could tell what was moved.

WHO GOES IN THE HOUSE?

Work with a partner.

1. People go in the house if they follow the rule. Otherwise they go in the yard. What is the rule in this picture?

2. Think of a rule. Use your rule to put some People in the house and some in the yard. Can your partner guess your rule?

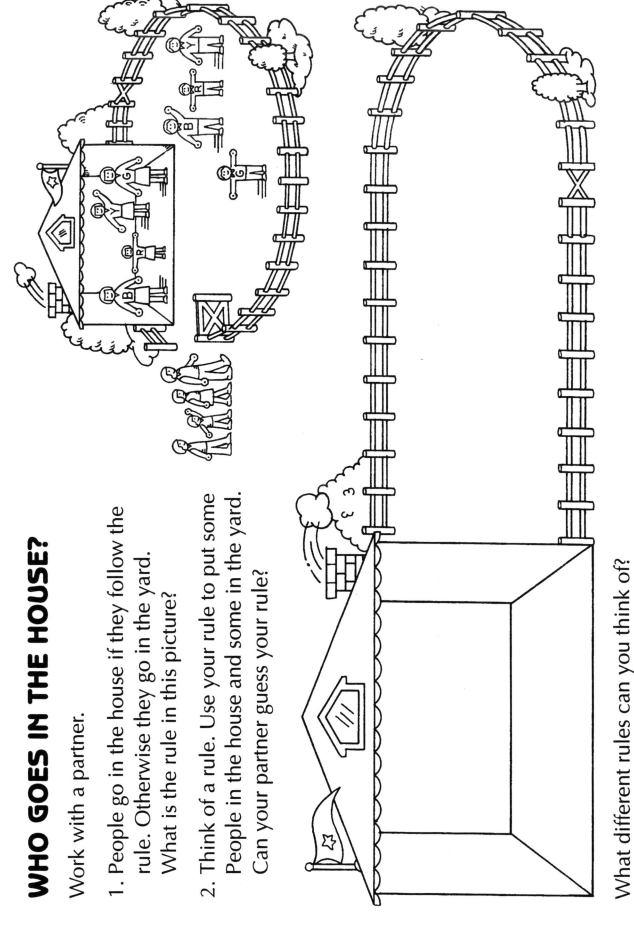

What different rules can you think of?

GROUPS OF PEOPLE

Work with a partner.

1. Here are two groups of Connecting People.

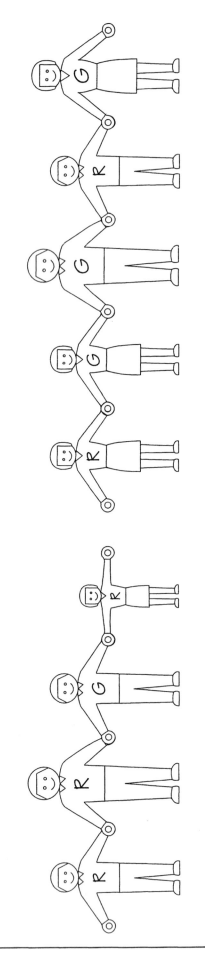

How are the groups alike? How are they different? List the ways.

2. Each of you make a group of People.
   One of you say something that is the same about the groups.
   The other say something that is different. Keep going as long as you can.

Try this again. Make two more groups of People. This time, switch roles.
Whoever said what was the same now say what was different.

DICE GAME

This is a game for 2 to 6 players. Take turns.
Put some Connecting People in the middle of the table.

1. On your turn, toss two dice. One should have numbers.
For the other die, choose

number

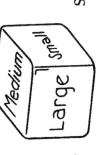

colors, or

male/female, or

size.

Take the People that match what your dice show.

For example, if you toss [blank], you can take any 4 red People.

2. If none of the People you need are left, you miss your turn.

3. Play until all the People are taken or until no one takes a person for two rounds.

The winner is the player with the most People at the end of the game.

How do you decide which die to take?

SPINNER GAME

This is a game for 2 to 6 players. Take turns.
Put some Connecting People in the middle of the table.

1. On your turn, toss a number die. The number tells you how many spinners to choose.

2. Spin your spinners. Take all People that your spinners show.

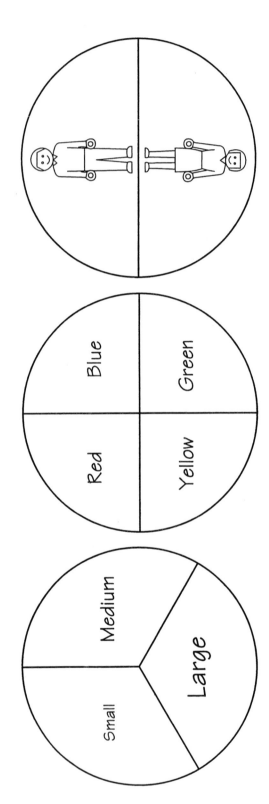

3. If none of the People you need are left, give one of your People back.

4. Play until all the People are taken *or* until no one takes a person for two rounds.

The winner is the player with the most People at the end of the game.

What is the best number to toss? How do you decide which spinners to use?

2 MAKING PATTERNS WITH CONNECTING PEOPLE

As soon as children discover how the hands of Connecting People can be joined, they make long rows of People holding hands. The rows invite questions about patterning. The five activities in this cluster explore some of these questions.

Before children begin structured activities with patterns, they should have had many informal experiences making patterns, using a variety of materials and describing the patterns. Young children usually create patterns as they play with construction materials such as blocks, and in their art work. You can draw children's attention to these patterns as well as to others in their environment in such things as clothing, wrapping paper, jewelry, and decorative arts. Children should realize that in these activities, the word "pattern" means more than just an arrangement. Here, pattern is a special kind of arrangement with a rule for how it can be duplicated or continued. The rule may call for simple repetition or it may dictate a progression or changing sequence based on mathematical or other relationships.

Children also experience patterns in sound and movement through music and dance activities. You can formalize and extend children's comprehension of such patterns by asking them to follow patterns in a song such as "Head and shoulders, knees and toes, knees and toes, . . . ," in which they repeatedly touch their body parts in order. You can also make a game of following patterns that you or they make up, such as "Clap your hands twice, touch your shoulders, clap your hands twice, touch your shoulders, ..." Many teaching activities of this sort, forming a gradual transition from motion and sound to manipulatives and drawings, are described in *Mathematics Their Way* by Mary Baratta-Lorton.

Connecting People are ideal for expanding on children's early work with repetitive patterns while encouraging them to look at more than one attribute at a time. In this cluster, children will need a large number of Connecting People, since they will probably be using several identical People when making patterns.

You may want children to record their patterns on strips of paper. Because children might find it difficult to draw the different People clearly, they may invent a code for the People, an important step in the development of symbolic language. Children can also use rubber stamps made to look like the People, or they can color, cut out, and paste copies of the People provided on page 76. A collection of pattern strips children have made can be used to raise their level of thinking about patterning by challenging them to compare and classify patterns in ways described below.

Work with patterns can involve interesting number challenges. For example, you might use two colors of Connecting People to show children two patterns to extend: one BAAABAAABAAA, the other BABAABAAABAAAA. Ask children which uses more As: a pattern extended to a row of 20 People or a pattern that reaches across a desktop. Patterns children create can be used to pose more challenges of this type.

HOLDING HANDS PAGE 25

Materials: A large number of Connecting People

Children are given a pattern to copy and extend. They take turns adding People to the row and describing the resulting pattern. Children then begin patterns individually, trade them, and see if they can continue a partner's pattern.

You might help children take turns to ensure that no one child's thinking dominates the activity. Be alert to the possibility that children may come up with more than one way to extend a given pattern. This idea is developed further in the activity *Making Patterns Grow.*

You can collect a set of patterning challenges by having children record the first 8 to 10 pieces in their patterns on a strip of paper using rubber stamps or cutout copies of the People. Later, other children can try to identify and continue the patterns on the strips.

When discussing children's patterns, you might introduce ideas of measurement and number by asking children to estimate how many People in a certain pattern will fit across their desk or if there will be more males or females in their pattern.

COMPARING PATTERNS PAGE 26

Materials: A large number of Connecting People

Children are asked to extend and compare two different patterns of Connecting People. They then create a new pattern and compare it to these two.

To introduce this activity, you might want to model some appropriate language for comparison of patterns. For example:

Is color used in the pattern? Which colors are used? How are they used?

Is a group of People repeated in the pattern? If so, how many People are used in the repeated group? What sizes are used? How are males and females used?

Be sure that children see several ways in which the two patterns are alike and several ways in which the two patterns are different. Discuss how similar patterns can also be represented with other materials or by using body motions, sounds, and so on.

If you ask children to record the patterns they make on strips of paper, the strips can be displayed on a bulletin board, perhaps using a "Guess My Rule" format for classifying them.

MAKING PATTERNS GROW PAGE 27

Materials: A large number of Connecting People

Children are given just four Connecting People in order to find at least two different patterns that begin with these People. They then repeat the activity using

---

Math With Connecting People™
© Learning Resources, Inc.

their own choice of four People. This activity helps students to see that a few examples don't necessarily establish a pattern (regardless of what some ill-conceived multiple-choice tests indicate).

Before starting, you might show children another beginning for a pattern and encourage them to come up with a wide variety of possible extensions. To allow children to focus on only one attribute, you may use simpler materials, such as chips or beads of two different colors. The first pattern could be ABAB. With this beginning, children might come up with the following possible patterns:

ABABABABABAB . . .

ABABBABBBABBBB . . .

ABABBABABBABABB . . .

ABABCABABCABABC . . .

Ask children to use words to describe the rule suggested by each of the patterns.

Encourage children to share their results and to search for new patterns that start from one another's choice of beginning People. Children should see that the search for patterns is really guesswork. No matter how many pieces are shown, one cannot be sure what will come next unless one is told something about the rule.

BREAK IN TWO, WHAT DID I DO? PAGE 28

Materials: A large number of Connecting People

Children make puzzles for each other by creating a pattern with Connecting People, breaking it into two parts, and putting it back together in the wrong order. They then give it to a partner with the challenge to find out where the puzzle was broken.

To introduce the activity, you might model how the *Break In Two, What Did I Do?* idea could work with a familiar pattern. For example:

1 2 3 4 5 6 7 8 9 10   can become   8 9 10 1 2 3 4 5 6 7

You could also do this physically with a colored pattern of interlocking cubes joined in a rod. Have children share their strategies for finding out where the pattern was broken. One strategy might be trial and error by simply trying to break the row in various places to see if a recognizable pattern is formed. Another strategy might be to start from either end and try to find a pattern, then note where it is broken. There may be more than one answer to a puzzle like this. The puzzle is easier if children make longer rows of People.

CHANGE THE PATTERN PAGE 29

Materials: A large number of Connecting People

Children learn to recognize and describe similarities among patterns by noting how one pattern can be transformed into another by following rules about changing specific attributes such as color, size, or gender. Children will discover that when patterns are changed, certain aspects remain the same, for example, the length of a part that is repeated—if it is a repeating pattern—or the presence of identical People in the pattern.

If you have assembled a collection of children's patterns recorded on strips of paper, you can challenge children to find a pair of patterns and a set of rules that transform one pattern into another. Using the same thinking, you might ask children to transform their patterns into other types of materials, into drawings, or into patterns of sound or movement.

HOLDING HANDS

Work with a partner.

1. Some Connecting People are holding hands in a pattern. Copy them with your People.
   Add on People to continue the pattern. Take turns.
   Add 6 more People altogether.
   Talk about the pattern with your partner.

2. Each of you make a new pattern with the People. Join their hands.
   Trade patterns. Try to continue your partner's pattern.
   Trade back. Did you agree?

How can you tell what will come next in a pattern?

COMPARING PATTERNS

1. Here are two patterns. What comes next in each pattern?

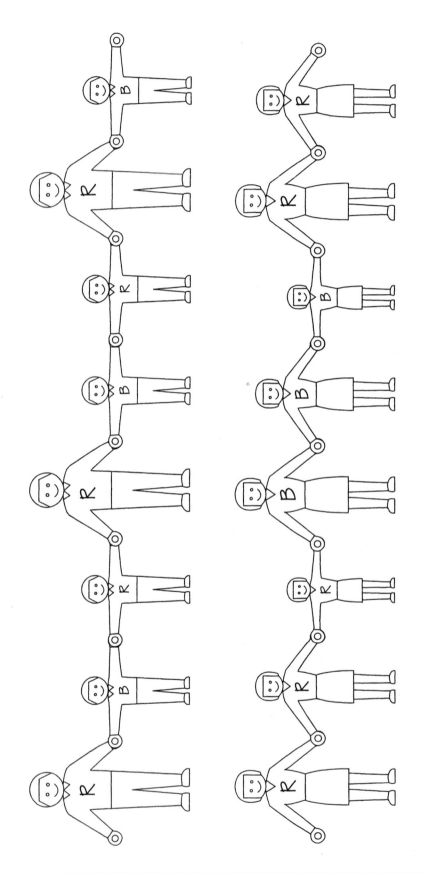

How are the two patterns alike? How are they different? List the ways.

2. Make a different pattern. Use just red and blue Connecting People. Join their hands.

How is your pattern like the two above? How is it different?

Math With Connecting People™
© Learning Resources, Inc.

MAKING PATTERNS GROW

1. Keisha and José made different patterns. Each had 10 Connecting People.
   Both patterns began like this.

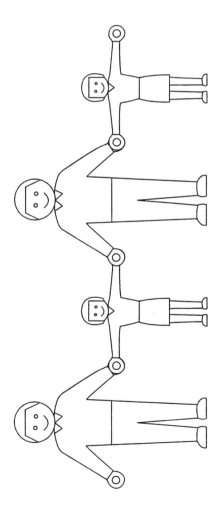

   What could Keisha's pattern have been?
   What could José's pattern have been?

2. Start a pattern. Use four Connecting People. Join their hands.
   Add more People to your pattern.
   Use the same beginning pattern to start two more patterns.

   How many People do you need to see before you know what the pattern is?

BREAK IN TWO, WHAT DID I DO?

Work with a partner.

1. Janet made a pattern of Connecting People holding hands.
   She dropped it on the floor and it broke into two pieces.
   Tracy put the two pieces back together, but switched the two parts.
   This is what they looked like.

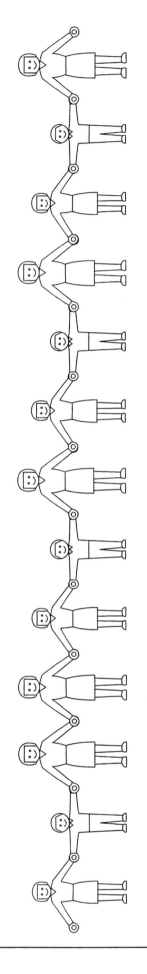

Can you tell where the pattern was broken?
Show how the People looked before Janet dropped them.

2. Each of you make a new pattern with 10 People. Join their hands.
   Break the pattern and switch the two parts.

Trade patterns. Can you tell where the pattern was broken?
How can you tell?

CHANGE THE PATTERN

1. Here is a pattern made with Connecting People.

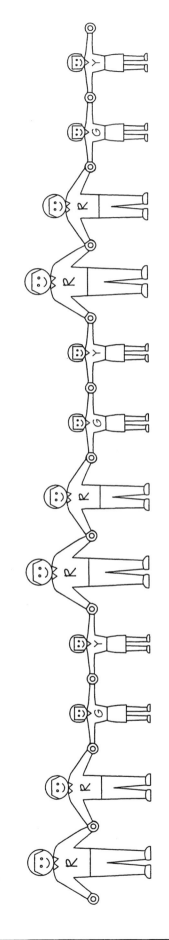

Make another pattern like this one. This time change the rule.
Change every male to a female and every female to a male.
This is one way to show that rule.

male → female, female → male

2. Change the first pattern again. This time use this rule.

red → green, medium → small

How are the three patterns alike? How are they different?

3. Make up your own rule for changing the pattern.
Copy the first pattern and then change it. Use your rule.

Show your pattern to a classmate.
Can he or she tell what rule you used?

---

3 TELLING PEOPLE STORIES

When children play with Connecting People, they start to tell stories about them and to embroider on their characteristics as people. The five activities in this cluster build on this tendency to tell stories. The People are used to act out various numerical/logical relations.

The human qualities of the Connecting People will make them useful in your classroom in many ways. You might give each pair of children a few People to use in acting out verbal number stories that you or other children tell. For example: "I went for a walk with three of my friends. In the park we met two more friends. One person had to go home for lunch. How many of us were there then?" The People are also appealing as markers in games or to use on a number line.

WHAT CAN WE PLAY?   PAGE 34

Materials: A large number of Connecting People

Certain children's games require fixed numbers of players. "Catch" requires two while "Monkey in the Middle" requires three. Here, children take a handful of People and see which activities can be done by everyone, with no one left out when games require 2, 3, 4, or 5 people.

Essentially, children are learning the concept of division, with and without remainder, although the language need not be formalized at this level. You can introduce this activity using the children as a context. Ask children if they think the class can be split up into pairs to play a 2-player game. Have them try it. Ask if the class could be grouped by threes for a 3-player game and so forth. Help children understand that their solution to the first part of the game requires them to divide a handful of Connecting People into groups of a certain size. With certain numbers such as 7, 11, and 13, children will discover that the answer to the question "What game can everyone play?" is "None."

In the second part of the activity, children will need 20 People to play "Catch," "Board Game," and "Toss in the Blanket," but not "Monkey in the Middle" (20 is divisible by 2, 4 and 5 but not 3). The third part has no solution. If the People can be arranged into groups of 4, they can also be arranged into groups of 2—any number divisible by 4 is also divisible by 2. An additional challenge is to find a number of People that can be grouped to do any of these activities. This will require a common multiple of 2, 3, 4 and 5, or 60 at a minimum!

· The same type of activity can be used to develop understanding of place value. On slips of paper, you can draw outlines of "buses" in which each bus has 10 spaces. Have children take a handful of Connecting People and estimate how many they are holding. They then arrange them in the buses and use the number of buses (e.g. 2) and the number of People left over (e.g. 6) to determine how many

People there are in all (26). Young children may also want to count the People to verify the amount.

TWO FRIENDS PAGE 35

Materials: Connecting People

Children are given a riddle with clues about a pair of People. They find Connecting People that satisfy all the clues. Children are encouraged to find more than one solution and then make up their own riddles for each other.

To introduce the use of varied clues to figure out who the People could be, you might play "Twenty Questions." Tell children that you are holding one person in your hand. Challenge them to find out which it is by asking Yes-No questions. This game encourages children to listen to one another and to put together information from earlier questions. When children have mastered this game, try it with two People—a more complex challenge.

When children have done the first part, encourage them to share their strategies for using the clues. They might look at the last three clues and remove all of the males, all the large People, and all the red and yellow People. The first two clues tell children that one friend must be medium and the other small and that one must be green and the other blue. The two possibilities are a medium green female and a small blue female or a medium blue female and a small green female. You might ask children how one clue could be changed so that there is only one solution.

If children record their own sets of clues on file cards, these can be added to a classroom file of Connecting People riddles.

LINING UP PAGE 36

Materials: Connecting People, at least one of each type

In this activity, clues involve relative position as well as the characteristics of the People. Children are given clues about four Connecting People who are in line. As in the previous activity, children first use the pieces to solve a given riddle, then they make up their own riddle.

Encourage children to share their strategies after doing the first part. They might begin by removing all the red People. The second person is determined by the fourth clue. The two small girls must be in the third and fourth positions since they are together in line. Because the last person must be green, the third must be yellow. Finally, the first person must be the large yellow female. This riddle has only one solution, but many riddles that children make up will have multiple solutions.

WALKING HOME   PAGE 37

Materials: Connecting People, two of a single color per player; two number dice—one red, one green

"Walking Home" is a game for 2 to 4 players. It gives experience moving backwards and forwards on a number line, laying the foundation for understanding this model for addition and subtraction. It also involves reasoning, since children will develop strategies for deciding how to move. You can create red and green dice by coloring a standard white dice with markers.

To prepare children, demonstrate the game moves by having each child draw a number line from 1 to 10 and then "walk" a Connecting person along this line according to certain directions.

For example, if a person starts at 5, show where he or she will be by walking 3 spaces to the right, or 2 spaces to the left. If appropriate, encourage children to predict where the person will end up before they try it. Depending on children's prior experience with the operations of addition and subtraction, you may want to make the connection explicit—that is, moving to the right corresponds to addition, moving to the left corresponds to subtraction.

Allow children to play this game several times. Discuss with them the choices they make. In particular, ask them to think about which are the best places to put a person when children have the choice. Are there any positions from which a person cannot get "Home?" Do you actually have to count out all the spaces indicated by the dice or can you take shortcuts?

Encourage children to try varying the rules of this game. What happens if you change the numbers on the dice? What else could you change? (The length of the board? The number of Connecting People used?)

CIRCUS TICKETS   PAGE 38

Materials: Connecting People; play money (one- and five-dollar bills—optional)

Children are shown a price list for circus tickets for the Connecting People. The price of each ticket depends on the size of the person. First, children figure out how much tickets will cost for a collection of People. Then they find other groups of People whose tickets will cost the same amount, with either more or fewer People. Children may find it helpful to use play money.

This activity allows for a variety of problem-solving challenges. Children might approach the first part by trial and error, but they might also use reasoning. Three dollars will buy one ticket for a medium person or three tickets for a small person. So 3 small People can take the place of 1 medium person without changing the cost. Likewise, $5 will buy a ticket for 1 large person or a ticket for 1 medium and 2 small People.

Math With Connecting People™
© Learning Resources, Inc.

The second part has many solutions. If children find one solution by trial and error, they might find others by reasoning. They may find that tickets for 4 large people and 6 small People cost $26. They might then reason that tickets for 1 large and 1 small person cost the same as the tickets for 2 medium People; hence, 2 medium People can be substituted for 1 large and 1 small person without changing the total cost of the tickets. If children make this substitution several times, they will find other solutions. They may notice patterns by making a table summarizing their work.

Size of person Cost of ticket	Large $5	Medium $3	Small $1
Number of each ticket that $26 will buy	4	0	6
	3	2	5
	2	4	4
	1	6	4
	0	8	2

Most puzzles that students create will have multiple solutions. You might vary this activity by having only two prices: $5 for large or medium and $3 for small. In this case, a problem such as "Eight People paid $34 for their tickets. How many small People were there?" has only one solution.

If students write their responses to the last part on file cards, you can assemble them to form a set of problems for the class.

WHAT CAN WE PLAY?

Here are some games that Connecting People like to play.

Catch
takes 2 people

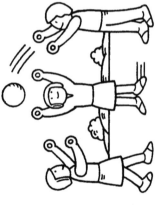

Monkey in the Middle
takes 3 people

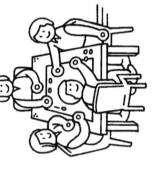

Board Game
takes 4 people

Toss in the Blanket
takes 5 people

1. Take a handful of Connecting People. They all want to play the same game together at the same time. What game can everyone play? Write down what you find out. Try this two more times.

2. Can you gather a group of People who could play every game together but **Monkey in the Middle?** How many People would be in your group?

3. Can you gather a group who could play **Monkey in the Middle** together and then **Board Games** but not **Catch?** How many People would be in your group?

TWO FRIENDS

Work with a partner.

1. Two friends went for a walk. Here are some clues about them.

   • They are not the same size.

   • They are not the same color.

   • Both are female.

   • Neither of them is large.

   • Neither of them is red or yellow.

   Find Connecting People who could be these two friends.
   You and your partner describe them.
   Are there two other People who fit all the clues?

2. Pick two People and write some clues about them.
   Don't let your partner see.
   Trade clues. Find two People who match all your partner's clues.
   Is there another solution?

LINING UP

Work with a partner.

1. Four People are in line. Here are some clues about them.

- None are red.

- The only green person is last.

- No one is next to someone of the same color.

- The second person is a large blue male.

- Two small girls are together.

- One person is a large female.

Find Connecting People who could be these four people. Describe them.
Is there another solution?
Are there four other People who fit all the clues?

2. Pick four People and write some clues about them.
Don't let your partner see.
Trade clues. Find four People who match all your partner's clues.
Is there another solution?

WALKING HOME

This is a game for 2 to 4 players. Take turns.
Each player picks a different color. Choose either red, green, blue, or yellow.
Each player takes two Connecting People of that color and puts them anywhere on the board below.

1. On your turn, toss two dice. One should be green, the other red.
   The green die shows how many spaces to move one of your People to the right.
   The red die shows how many spaces to move one of your People to the left.
   Try to make both moves.

2. If you cannot make *both* moves, leave your People where they are and miss a turn.

3. When one of your People lands on Home, you get 1 point.
   Put the person back anywhere on the board. Go on playing.

The winner is the first one to get 4 points.

◄── RED   GREEN ──►

HOME	1	2	3	4	5	6	7	8	9	10	11	12	13	14	HOME

CIRCUS TICKETS

Connecting People are going to the circus!
Here is a price list for tickets.

TICKET PRICES

Large $5.00
Medium $3.00
Small $1.00

1. Take a handful of Connecting People. How many did you take?
   How much will circus tickets cost for all these People?
   Find fewer People whose tickets cost the same amount.
   Find more People whose tickets cost the same amount.

2. A group of 10 People paid 26 dollars. Find 10 People whose tickets
   would cost 26 dollars. Can you do it another way? A third way?

3. Make up a problem for a classmate to try.
   Take some People and count them. Figure out how much their tickets would cost.
   Tell a classmate how many People you have and how much the tickets cost.
   Can he or she find People who fit your problem? Were their sizes the same as yours?

Math With Connecting People™
© Learning Resources, Inc.

4 CLASSIFYING CONNECTING PEOPLE

During free exploration, most children arrange the Connecting People into groups by color, size, or gender. The following five activities build on this natural tendency to sort. The first activity leads children to design puzzles for each other based on numerical relations. The other four, which use loops to describe classification schemes, provide a context for the development of logical language and for problem solving. Children should have had prior experience with classifying and describing the People in free play and/or in the activities *Who Goes in the House?*, *Dice Game,* and *Spinner Game.*

Any assortment of Connecting People could be used for these activities. However, when using an attribute set of 24 Connecting People for the loop activities, children can check their arrangements by counting and can explore interesting numerical challenges.

TAKE TEN   PAGE 43

Materials: Connecting People

Children select ten Connecting People and sort them by gender, size, and color. For each way of sorting children write a number sentence—a sum of two, three, or four numbers, all equal to 10. Children then are given the much more difficult challenge of doing this process backwards.

To introduce the activity, demonstrate how to sort a collection of Connecting People by attribute and write a number sentence for each way of sorting. You might want to use a number other than 10 for this demonstration. Be sure that children realize that the numbers in the sums may be zero.

In the second part, children may need encouragement to experiment, to guess a solution, and to check it. Have children share their various strategies, successful or not. One approach is to look at just one number sentence and collect 4 females and 6 males to match the sentence $4 + 6 = 10$. Probably the other two number sentences won't fit. You can start, however, by replacing People— changing color or size but not gender—to make the collection fit the next sentence. Through this activity children can learn the value of getting something partially right and then finding a way to correct what is wrong. They should also realize that there are many possible solutions to this challenge. A further benefit is that children get a lot of experience with different ways to break 10 into sums, which can be very helpful as they learn basic facts of addition. You can collect the number sentences children wrote to add to a file of student-written Connecting People problems. Children might try varying the number of Connecting People they start with.

LOOPS PAGE 44

Materials: Connecting People; two pieces of yarn about 60 cm long tied into loops; four color labels, and three size labels (see page 77)

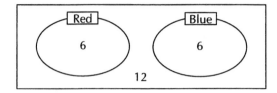

This activity establishes the language of loops (also known as Venn diagrams) as a way to describe classification. Children arrange Connecting People so that each piece within a given loop has the characteristic specified by the loop's label and each piece outside the loop does not. Each child then takes a loop, labeled with different colors, and works cooperatively to place all the People so that they satisfy the requirements of both loops. Children find that if they have a representative sample of Connecting People, the two loops will have about the same number of People in them while the area outside will have about twice as many. (If they work with an attribute set of 24 People, the numbers will be as shown.) Make sure that children realize what it means for People to be placed in the region outside the loops—that is, those People are neither of the colors on the labels of the two loops. In this example, they are neither red nor blue.

In the second part, if children select "Small" and "Red," for example, they will find that if the loops are separate from each other, placing all the red People in one loop means they can't place all the small People in the other loop. Some of the red People are also small, and some of the small People are also red. Give children plenty of time to explore this problem. When the loops are moved so that they overlap, all the Connecting People can be placed as shown. Don't let children see this arrangement until they realize the problem and have had a chance to come up with a solution. If they use an attribute set of 24 Connecting People, they will find that the numbers in each region are as shown. Lead children to discover the need for an overlap for some labels.

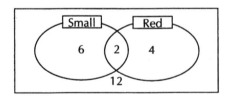

LABELS ON LOOPS PAGE 45

Materials: Connecting People; two pieces of yarn about 60 cm long tied into loops; four color labels, three size labels, and two gender labels (see page 77)

Children are asked to copy an arrangement of overlapping loops with labels and a few People placed in them, and finish sorting the People into the loops or on the outside. Children then can solidify their understanding of the language of loops

---

when one child moves a piece while the others close their eyes and try to figure out what was moved. Finally, children pick other labels for the loops and play the same game with their own arrangements.

This activity provides children with further opportunities to deepen their understanding of using loops for classification. Encourage children to experiment with labels and to talk about their discoveries and strategies.

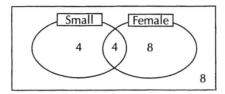

Demonstrate "What Did I Do?" and have children share their thinking about how to figure out what was moved. Be sure children realize that they must check both what is inside and what is outside each loop. Children may want to make this game more competitive, perhaps rewarding the first person to see what was moved. The reward may be a point or the chance to be the next one to do the moving. Be aware that competition might discourage children who are slower to observe differences. You can downplay the emphasis on speed by asking children to raise their hands but not say out loud which piece was moved. Or perhaps they can write or draw their answer on paper. This gives all children time to think.

To extend this activity, you can ask children to use an attribute set of 24 Connecting People and keep track of the numbers in each region in their arrangements. They will find there are only a limited number of combinations of numbers: {9,3,3,9}, {8,4,4,8}, {6,2,4,12}, {6,0,6,12}, {8,0,8,8}, {12,0,12,0}, {8,0,16,0}, and {6,0,18,0}.

You might give children one set of numbers like this and challenge them to find labels for loops so that these numbers are in each region.

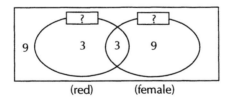

(red)   (female)

A further extension is to introduce negative labels such as "Not Red" or "Not Small." Children should understand the meaning of a double negative—if a person is *not* in a loop labeled "Not Red," that person must be red.

GUESS THE LABELS   PAGE 46

Materials: Connecting People; two pieces of yarn about 60 cm long tied into loops; four color labels, three size labels, and two gender labels (see page 77)

Children guess labels for two overlapping loops by examining a few Connecting People placed in the loops. In so doing, children experience the process of forming and verifying hypotheses while also developing their ability to think simultaneously about more than one attribute of an object. Children choose their own labels, place People in the loops, then hide the labels and guess each other's labels.

To begin, remind children of the activity *Who Goes in the House?* Then play a "Guess My Rule" game using one loop instead of the image of a house and yard. To do this with a whole class (up to 24 students), split the group into two teams. The teams line up on either side of a loop of yarn on the floor. Think of a rule, but don't tell the children. Each child takes a Connecting person. Players from the front of each line take turns placing their pieces in the arrangement—either inside or outside the loop. If their placement is correct, tell them so, then have them leave their pieces in the arrangement, and sit down. If they are not correct, they keep their piece and return to the back of the line. The team whose members all sit down first wins. Children may enjoy this type of competition, but downplay it if some children are made uncomfortable. Later, for further challenge, use two overlapping loops in the game.

The second part of this activity works well if several groups do it at the same time. Each group selects its own labels for the loops, places Connecting People in the loops, and turns the labels over so they can't be read. Groups can then go and look at the arrangements of the other groups and try to guess their labels.

THREE LOOPS   PAGE 47

Materials: Connecting People; three pieces of yarn about 60 cm long tied into loops; four color labels, three size labels, and two gender labels (see page 77)

This activity extends work with two loops to three loops, and should not be attempted until children are comfortable with placement of pieces in two-loop arrangements. Part 2, which resembles the *Guess the Labels* activity, works well if several groups are doing it simultaneously so they can share their work.

For further challenges, children can use negative labels such as "Not Red." You can also challenge children to find labels so that certain areas have no pieces in them. For example, if shading means that no pieces are to be placed in the area and no shading means that at least one piece is placed in the area, ask children to find labels that yield the following situations. (Possible labels for the three loops are given below each diagram.) Children then create their own labels for the loops, turn them over, and ask a classmate to guess what they say.

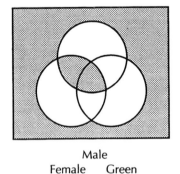

Male
Female   Green

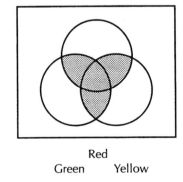

Red
Green   Yellow

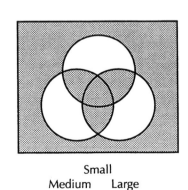

Small
Medium   Large

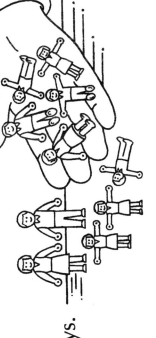

TAKE TEN

Work with a partner.

1. Take 10 Connecting People. Sort them in three different ways.
   Write an addition sentence for each way.
   Some of the numbers in the sentences may be 0.

Here are some examples.

Sort by male-female. You might write ———→ $4 + 6 = \underline{10}$

Sort by size. You might write ———→ $5 + 2 + 3 = \underline{10}$

Sort by color. You might write ———→ $0 + 3 + 2 + 5 = \underline{10}$

2. Find 10 People who would give these sentences.
   $4 + 6 = 10$ $1 + 5 + 4 = 10$ $3 + 0 + 5 + 2 = 10$

3. Trade number sentences with your partner.
   Look for 10 People to show your partner's sentences.
   Are they the same People as your partner's?

LOOPS

Work with a partner.

1. Each of you take a loop of yarn. Put a different color label on each loop.

| Blue | Green | Yellow |

Put every person that matches a label inside its loop. Put every person that does not match a label outside.

Where are the most People? Are there more in your loop, your partner's loop, or outside?

2. This time, one of you take a label for size and the other take a label for color.

| Small | Medium | Large |

| Red | Blue | Yellow | Green |

Can you place all the People so that they are all where they belong?

Talk with your partner about what you discover.

Red

LABELS ON LOOPS

Work in a group of 2 to 4.

1. Copy this picture with loops and Connecting People. Put the rest of the People where they belong. Place them in the loops or on the outside.

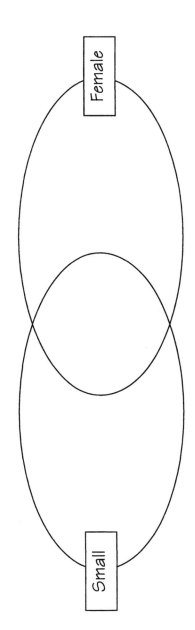

2. Play "What Did I Do?" All but one player close their eyes. That player moves one Connecting Person to a different area. The other players open their eyes. They try to find out which piece was moved.
Take turns moving the person.

3. Pick other labels for the loops. Place some People in the loops. Play "What Did I Do?" Here are some labels you might use.

Red	Yellow	Large
Blue	Small	Male
Green	Medium	Female

GUESS THE LABELS

1. Copy this picture with loops and Connecting People. What could the missing labels be?

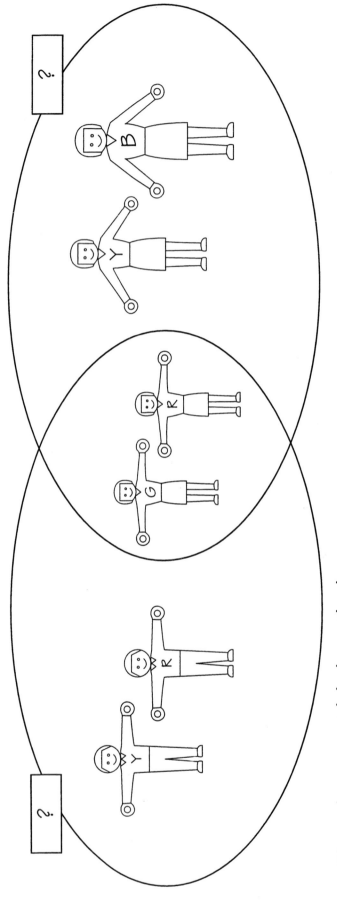
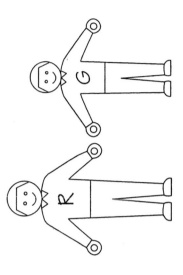

Place the correct labels on the loops.
Put the rest of the People in the loops or outside.

2. Remove the People and labels.
Pick your own labels for the loops. Place all the People in the loops or outside. Turn over your labels.

Ask a classmate to guess what they say.

THREE LOOPS

1. Copy this picture with loops and Connecting People. What could the missing labels be?

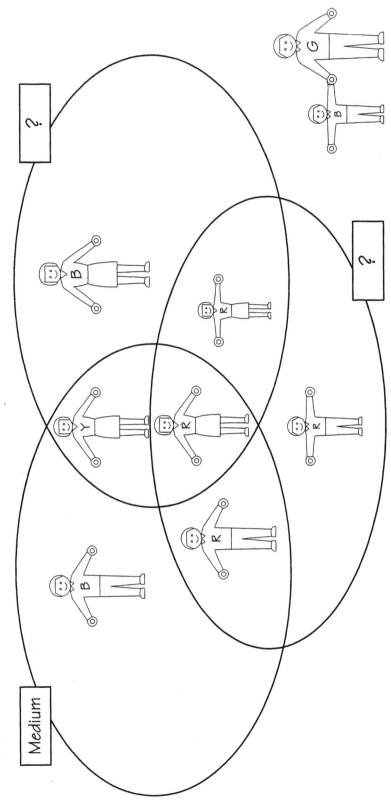

Place the correct labels on the loops. Put the rest of the People in the loops or outside.

2. Remove the People and labels from your three loops.
   Pick your own labels for the loops. Place all the People in the loops or outside.
   Turn over your labels.
   Ask a classmate to guess what they say.

5 USING AN ATTRIBUTE SET OF CONNECTING PEOPLE

Each of the following five activities requires an attribute set of Connecting People in which one of each type of person is represented. An attribute set has a mathematical structure that encourages logical thinking. Every possible combination of the attributes of color, size, and gender is represented, and there are no duplicates. Since there are 4 colors, 3 sizes, and 2 genders, this set has 4 x 3 x 2 = 24 Connecting People. Children may have been using attribute sets in early activities but have not directly explored their mathematical properties.

A way to introduce children to the structure of the attribute set is to give them a bag from which you have removed just one piece and challenge them to figure out what is missing. Encourage them to share their strategies for finding the missing piece. One approach is to sort by color and count the number of People in each group. Children will find that for three colors there are 6 People but for one color only 5. If they pair all the males and females of the same size in this color, they will find out who is missing. Another approach is to arrange the People in an array, perhaps with rows of the same size and columns of the same color.

Many attribute sets are available commercially. Sets most often used are those of common geometric shapes with attributes of color, shape, size, and thickness. Activities designed for other attribute sets can easily be adapted for use with Connecting People.

HOW MANY PEOPLE? PAGE 52

Materials: Connecting People; container (bag, box, or can) for the People

Children take some People from the container and figure out, without counting, how many People are left in the container. They then estimate and check by counting which of various sets have more People—small or female, red or large, and blue or yellow. Finally, children figure out how many People there would be if the set were changed in some way, for example, if there were one less or one more color.

Three types of tasks lead children to discover quantitative aspects of the attribute set. If children know that there are 24 People in the set, and if they are proficient with subtraction, they may do the first part of this activity by computation. But other types of reasoning are likely. Children may separate out all the People of one color and reason that there ought to be a male and a female of each size, making 6 of each color. They can then find out how many are missing of each color and add these numbers. Another approach is to set up an array, perhaps with rows of the same color and columns of the same size. There should be a male and a female for each color and size in the array. Children can simply count the empty spaces.

While some children might approach the second part using direct memory, it is more likely that they will use reasoning. For example, there are 2 small People (male and female) of each color, making 2 x 4 = 8 small People. But there are 3 female People (small, medium, and large) of each color, making 3 x 4 = 12 females. Another way to reason is that since one half of the People are female and one third are small, there are more female People than small People.

The third part suggests the "combinations" model for multiplication that children will later learn more formally. If, for example, 5 colors and 3 sizes are available, there are 5 x 3 possible combinations of color and size. In this context children can think concretely and not in terms of multiplication as an operation. For instance, to figure out the number of combinations if there were also an orange color in the set, children can simply count one color over again.

ONE-DIFFERENCE LINEUPS   PAGE 53

Materials: Connecting People

Children copy and add specified People to a one-difference lineup. Children then play a game in which they take turns trying to add People to either end of a one-difference lineup.

The first part of this activity involves trial and error because children may get stuck if they try adding certain People in certain positions. The activity requires children to classify the same piece in more than one way. When children have completed *How Many Differences?*, they can return to this activity, repeating it for two- or three-difference lineups.

ONE-DIFFERENCE LOOPS   PAGE 54

Materials: Connecting People

Children are shown a loop with three gaps. They copy the loop and find People to fill the gaps. They then do the more open challenge—to use the entire attribute set to make a one-difference loop.

This activity builds on the previous one, but here the one-difference lineups must close up in a loop, adding an additional challenge. Children can use a variety of strategies to make a one-difference loop using all 24 pieces in the attribute set. Some children will build a lineup as long as they can and when they get stuck, will modify the ends to make it close it up. A more systematic approach is to first use all the females—small, then medium, then large, each time going through four colors—and then do a similar pattern with the males. If children use this approach, the final challenge will be easy for them since they can see that if one person is removed there will still be a one-difference loop.

As an extension, children might try this activity with other configurations, such as a figure eight. They might also try to make two- and three-difference loops. They may be surprised to find that if one person is removed from the attribute set, the remaining 23 People cannot be formed into a three-difference loop. In such a loop the People must alternate male and female, which requires an even number of People. Children might also try to make a one-difference loop using only a randomly selected handful of Connecting People.

HOW MANY DIFFERENCES? PAGE 55

Materials: Connecting People

Children compare each person in the attribute set to a given person and sort the set according to the number of ways in which each is different from the given person.

This activity gives children experience in noting similarities and differences between Connecting People and also helps them discover an interesting numerical pattern. In the first part, children should find that there are 6 People who are different in one way, 11 who are different in two ways, and 6 who are different in three ways. In the second part, children should discover that the numbers 6, 11 and 6 are always the same, no matter which person they start with. This can be explained by noting that to find a person different in just one way, changing just color gives 3 People, changing just size gives 2 People, or changing just gender gives 1 person, yielding $3 + 2 + 1 = 6$ People who are different in one way. On the other hand, a person who is different in all three ways must have one of the 3 different colors, one of the 2 different sizes, and a different gender, yielding $3 \times 2 \times 1 = 6$ People who are different in three ways. All the others will be different in two ways. When children are adept at noting the number of differences between two Connecting People, they can repeat the previous two "one-difference" activities for two and three differences, as noted above.

FOOTPRINT PUZZLES PAGE 56

Materials: Connecting People

Children put People on "footprints" so that the number of parallel lines between the footprints corresponds to the number of differences among the People standing there.

This activity introduces a logic puzzle involving differences among Connecting People. Puzzles like this are easy for children to design but can be surprisingly difficult to solve. To introduce the activity, show children how a puzzle can be designed, perhaps using only 3 or 4 Connecting People. Take the People off this puzzle and make a different one. By now children may have forgotten the actual placements on the first puzzle, so you can discuss how to go about solving it using trial and error.

Footprint puzzles are sometimes easier to solve if you know which Connecting People to use. For the example here, you might tell children to use only the People shown in the solution. (There are many other solutions.)

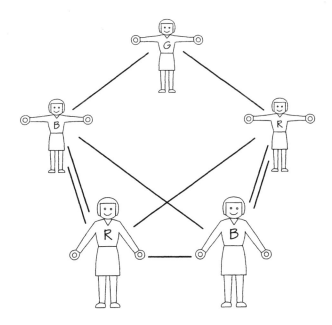

When children make their own puzzles, you might ask them to draw the footprints on large file cards, and record on the back which pieces they used to create the puzzle. They could draw the People, invent some sort of symbols for them, use rubber stamps, or make cutouts from copies of the People provided on page 76. A child doing the puzzle who needs a hint can turn the card over and select that set of People to try.

Discuss with children what makes these puzzles easy or difficult. In general puzzles are more difficult if a given person has to meet several criteria—for instance, the two lower People in the example on the activity page each have to be compared with two other People. A file of such puzzles in your classroom can provide many hours of enrichment and logical thinking.

HOW MANY PEOPLE?

You will need a container with a special set of Connecting People that has exactly one of each type of person.

1. Take a handful of Connecting People.
   Do not count how many are left in the container.
   Look at the People you took out.
   How many do you think are still in the container?
   Why do you think so? Count and see.

2. Answer these questions about all the People in the special set without looking.
   • Which are there more of, small People or female People?
   • Which are there more of, red People or large People?
   • Which are there more of, blue People or yellow People?
   • Why do you think so? Count and see.

3. How many People would there be if...
   • all the blue People disappeared?
   • a new group of orange People joined the set?
   • there were one more size?

Math With Connecting People™
© Learning Resources, Inc.

ONE-DIFFERENCE LINEUPS

Work in a group of 2 to 4.

1. This is called a 1-difference lineup.
   Each pair of neighbors is different *in just one way*. They may be different just by color, or by size, or by gender.

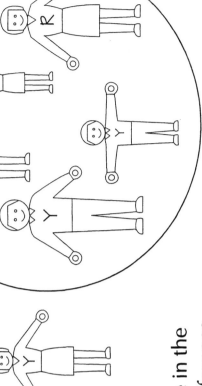

Copy this lineup with your People. Add the People in the loop to either end. Make sure you still have a 1-difference lineup when you are done.

2. Play this game. Share the set of Connecting People. Take turns.
   - The first player puts a person on the table to start a lineup.
   - Each player then must add a person to make a 1-difference lineup. Add to either end.
   - A player who cannot add a person is out of the game.
   - The winners are players who add a person every time it is their turn.

ONE-DIFFERENCE LOOPS

You will need a special set of Connecting People.

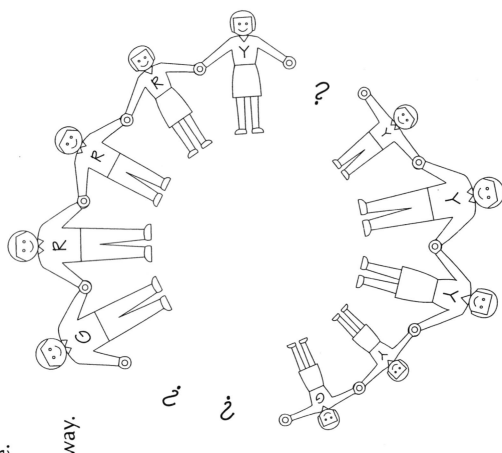

1. This is called a 1-difference loop.
   Each pair of neighbors is different in just one way.
   Three Connecting People are missing.
   Copy the loop with your People.
   Find 3 more People to fill in the gaps.

2. Use all 24 People in your set to make
   a 1-difference loop.

3. Take away 1 of the People. Could you
   still make a 1-difference loop? Try it.

Talk with classmates about what you discover.

HOW MANY DIFFERENCES?

1. Put the small blue girl in the footprints below. Sort the rest of the Connecting People into three piles.
   One pile needs People that are different from the girl in just one way.
   The second pile needs People that differ in two ways.
   The third pile needs People that differ in three ways.

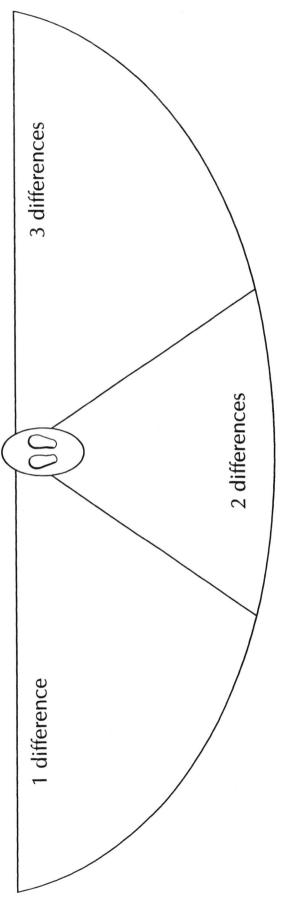

1 difference

2 differences

3 differences

Count how many People are in each pile.

2. Choose a different person to use in place of the small blue girl.
   Sort the rest of the People into three piles again.
   Count how many are in each pile. What do you notice?

FOOTPRINT PUZZLES

You can use lines to show differences between pairs of Connecting People. Here are examples.

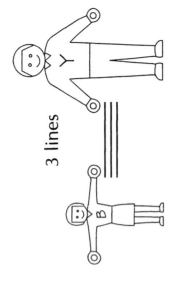

1 line

The one difference is color.

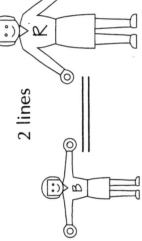

2 lines

The two differences are color and size.

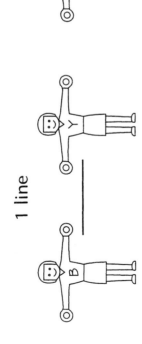

3 lines

The three differences are color, size, and gender

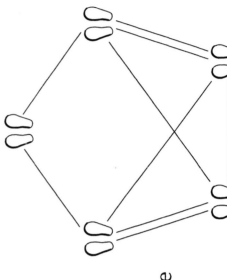

1. Try this puzzle. Put People on the footprints so that the lines show how many differences there are between pairs.

2. Make up your own puzzle. Draw some footprints and put People on them. Draw in lines to show how many differences there are between some pairs of the People. Take the People off and see if someone else can find People who solve your puzzle.

6 MEASURING WITH CONNECTING PEOPLE

The Connecting People vary in size, yet a set contains many People of identical sizes. This means that children can use the People to develop the concept of measurement as comparison of an object to be measured with multiple copies of the same unit. Children can also explore the effect of using different-size People as the unit of measurement—different measurements result. In the following five activities, children use the People to explore length, area, and weight.

If you listen to children's observations about the People during free exploration, you will probably hear them talk of size—small, medium, large, littlest, biggest, middle-size. Try to refine this language. Encourage children to describe in what ways the People vary in size. Although heights differ, the distance from hand to hand is approximately the same. Once children have noticed this, you can ask them to estimate how many People with joined hands it will take to fit across their desk. They can then snap the People together to check.

MAKE FIVE, FIND TWENTY   PAGE 61

Materials: A large number of Connecting People, including all sizes

Children draw a line they think is as long as 5 People joined hand to hand. They check the line with the Connecting People, look around the room to find something that will measure 20 People, and check their estimates. Finally, they choose their own lengths to measure and record their estimates and the actual measures on a chart. This activity helps to develop number sense and intuition about how number and length relate to the physical environment.

Children use the Connecting People as nonstandard units for measurement, which allows them to see the importance of having a standard unit. It shows children how different units lead to different measures—an important preparation for children who will need to measure in both inches and centimeters. Children may be challenged to see if it makes a difference if they use small, medium, or large People. Although it is difficult to compare the hand-to-hand length of individual People, it is easy to compare the lengths of rows of 10 People joined hand to hand. Encourage children to experiment with ways to compare the hand-to-hand length of small, medium, and large People. This activity allows children to come up with varied strategies for estimating. When they are looking for something as long as 20 People, they may notice how 5 is related to 20—that it is four times as much. Encourage children to use measurements they already have to help them make new estimates.

As an extension, children can play an estimation game. Have them take turns naming a classroom object and a part of it to measure, for example, the height of the wastebasket. Each child writes down a "People-length" estimate for the named object. The child that named the object measures it, and everyone writes the difference between their estimate and the actual length. At the end of several rounds, children add up these differences. The player with the smallest sum wins.

WHICH IS MORE? PAGE 62

Materials: A large number of Connecting People, including all sizes

Children make comparisons based on estimating and then measuring Connecting People in various positions and contexts.

This activity leads children to see many ways in which the People can be measured and can be used to measure. Children may develop and apply intuitive ideas of ratio. For example, since the small People are a little more than half as tall as the large People, one would expect that a row of 10 small People head to toe would be longer than a row of 5 large People head to toe.

Encourage children to come back to this activity after they have done *Weighing People* so that they can incorporate weight in their comparison questions. You can also provide models of questions that involve other materials, such as money. For example, "Which would you rather have, a stack of nickels as high as a medium person, or a stack of dimes as tall as a small person?" Children might find it amusing to apply some questions like these to themselves as well as to Connecting People.

Comparisons that children have designed can make interesting daily estimation challenges. You might pose such a comparison challenge at the start of the day, allowing children to choose an answer, and then check at the end of the day. Children will doubtless enjoy coming up with a comparison challenge that stumps many of their classmates.

PLACES TO LIVE PAGE 63

Materials: A large number of Connecting People; milk cartons or shoe boxes, food containers, match boxes, toothpick boxes, small gift boxes; light cardboard; tape; scissors

Children construct and furnish a room for some Connecting People out of milk cartons and other materials.

The Connecting People provide a natural context for building to scale. Before beginning this activity, you might ask children to bring some of the boxes needed to school. Emphasize that you will need boxes of many different sizes, specifying which kinds. When the boxes have been collected, ask children which ones could be used by the Connecting People as houses, rooms, or furniture. Then introduce the more specific challenge of the activity—to find a box suitable for a room, or for furniture. This activity motivates and develops careful measurement skills. It is easier for children to start with a solid shell, but they can build boxes from scratch out of cardboard. You might show how simple boxes can be made by folding a rectangle of light cardboard and taping it to make a rectangular "tunnel." Close up one or both open ends by taping on rectangles of the appropriate size.

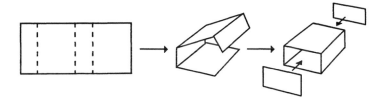

Children may use many strategies to choose dimensions for rooms and furniture. To design a bed, for example, they may look for a box whose length is an approximate match to the height of a person. The height of a bed is usually about the height of an adult's knee. Tables can be of various sizes, but their heights are a little less than half of an adult's height. To establish the height of the ceiling, children can compare their height to that of the classroom's ceiling, and then use a small person to establish the height of the ceiling in the People's room. Older children might measure actual dimensions of rooms, beds, and tables, and find how the heights of Connecting People compare to those of real people (a bit less than one thirtieth).

If children get involved in this project, it can be extended. Children might think about how to construct complete houses. They could try to build models of homes for the Connecting People that resemble their own. If there are no boxes of the right size, children may need to tape subdivisions into a large box. Stairs are also interesting to construct. Children might count the number of steps in a flight of stairs in the school and see how closely they should fold a strip of paper to get this many steps. Children could also assemble their various houses into a community and think of ways to design streets, sidewalks, and so forth.

SLEEPING IN TENTS   PAGE 64

Materials A large number of Connecting People, including at least 20 small People

Connecting People are going camping. Children are shown a rectangle representing the floor of a tent and indicate how many Connecting People can sleep in the tent, each in a sleeping bag. Children then draw a tent to hold 20.

This activity gives children experience with the concept of area. They will find that each person's sleeping bag occupies a rectangle of space, and that 8 of the

small People will fit in the tent, whereas only 6 of the large People will fit. In the second part, children think about how to arrange 20 small People to make a rectangle, which leads to finding factors of 20.

WEIGHING PEOPLE PAGE 65

Materials: A large number of Connecting People, including at least 10 large and 20 small People; a two-pan balance

Children have hands-on experiences with weighing and are asked to consider how the attributes of color, gender, and height relate to the weight of Connecting People.

Children are required to come up with strategies for comparing weights and for separating the variables. For example, they must consider just which People to put on the balance to see if yellow People weigh the same as red People. The two-pan balance will probably not show a difference in weight between, for instance, a large female and a large male, but it may pick up a difference if 10 of each of these are in the two pans of the balance. Children will find that color has no effect on weight, and that People of the same size of different genders have slightly different weights. Clearly, People of the same gender but different sizes weigh different amounts.

In the second part, children find that it takes more than 20 small People to balance 10 large People. But it only takes about 15 to match their height when put head to foot because when figures are enlarged, the volume increases much more than the height.

Math With Connecting People™
© Learning Resources, Inc.

MAKE FIVE, FIND TWENTY

1. Take one Connecting person. Look at it closely.
   Picture 5 People with their hands joined.
   Draw a line that you think is just as long.
   Join 5 People to check your line.

2. Look around the room. What is as long as 20 People with their hands joined?
   Check using the People.

3. Think of other things to measure. Fill in a chart.

	my arm					
Estimate						
Real number						

Do your estimates get better as you estimate and measure more things? Why?

WHICH IS MORE?

Take one Connecting person. Look at it closely. Answer these questions by estimating. Then use People to check.

Which is more...

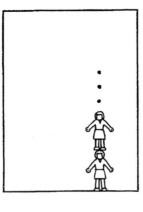

the number of small People joined hand to hand who can fit from top to bottom of your page,

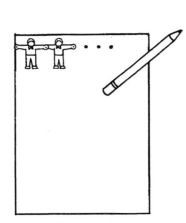

or the number of medium People lying head to toe needed to fit across your page?

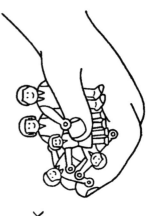

the number of People joined hand to hand who can fit from your elbow to your fingertip,

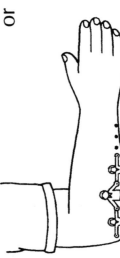

or the number of People you can pick up in your hand?

Think of some measurements to compare with Connecting People. First estimate and then measure.

Math With Connecting People™
© Learning Resources, Inc.

PLACES TO LIVE

You will need a large milk carton or shoe box, small boxes, scissors, tape, and light cardboard.

Pick a family of Connecting People. They need a place to live. Find a box that will make a comfortable room for them. Make sure the room is a good size. You may need to put a wall or a floor in the box.

Make or find boxes that could be tables, chairs, beds, or other furniture for the People.

How did you decide which boxes to use? Look at a classmate's room. Could it go with yours to be part of the same house?

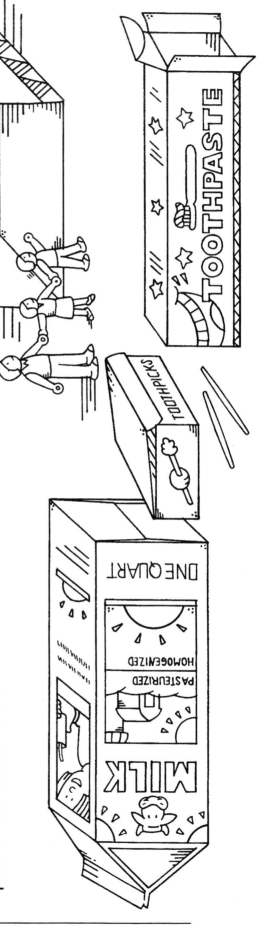

SLEEPING IN TENTS

1. The Connecting People are going camping.
   Here is the outline of the floor of their tent.
   Each person will sleep in a rectangular sleeping bag.
   How many small People can sleep in the tent?
   How many large People can sleep in the tent?

2. Draw the outline of the floor of another tent.
   The new tent should have a rectangle-shaped floor, also.
   It must hold 20 small People.

Math With Connecting People™
© Learning Resources, Inc.

WEIGHING PEOPLE

Work with a partner.

1. What do you think affects the weight of the Connecting People?

   Do you think color affects weight?
   Do you think gender affects weight?
   Do you think size affects weight?
   Use a two-pan balance to check your predictions.

2. How many small People weigh as much as 10 large People?
   How many small People head to toe are as long as 10 large People head to toe?

Are these two numbers the same? Can you explain?

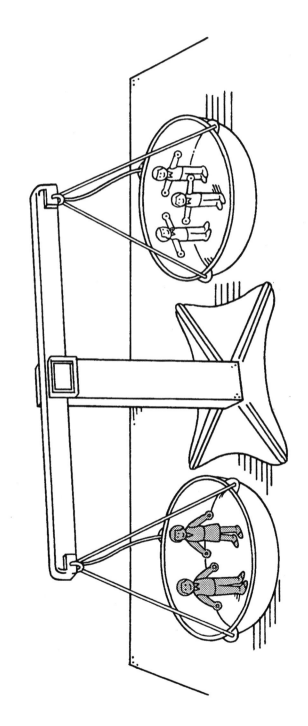

7 COLLECTING DATA ABOUT CONNECTING PEOPLE

Children need experience with formulating questions, collecting and analyzing data, and finding ways to describe their results both verbally and visually, as in graphs. The Connecting People provide a natural context for such experiences. The following five activities suggest various types of questions about the Connecting People that lead to the collection and analysis of data. Children sort and describe a large set of the People and estimate and count how many they can hold in a handful. They try to match a person by feel and experiment to see which People fall over most easily. Finally, children explore all possible combinations for two People of a specified type.

In many of these activities, previous experience with graphing is useful. For children who have not had such experience, you can try the following. Have each child select just one person and then estimate which color was chosen most by the class. Children will see that it is difficult to be sure just by looking around. Ask the children to move into groups according to the color they are holding. It is easier to count now, but it may not be immediately clear which color was chosen most. Finally, have children put their persons on a grid with four columns, labeled by color, to make a "concrete graph." Talk about the advantage of this type of display for telling which color was chosen most. To make a permanent record of this experience, children can make a bar graph by coloring in the squares in which each person is standing. This experience can be repeated as children sort the Connecting People by size or gender. Children should also make graphs about all sorts of other aspects of their environment.

CHOOSING PEOPLE   PAGE 70

Materials: Connecting People; graphs (see page 79—optional)

Children ask 20 individuals which of the 24 different Connecting People they would choose if they could have one piece to keep. Children then make a series of graphs to represent their findings.

If this activity is conducted in the school building, you might prepare a small tray with an attribute set of 24 Connecting People—one of each type—for children to show when they ask their "survey" question. To record answers to the question, children might write out the description in words, or they might invent some sort of code system such as S, M, and L, for the three sizes; R, B, Y, and G for the four colors; M and F for male and female. (The problem with using letters is that M stands for medium size and male. But if the position of the letter corresponds to an attribute—in a chart or in a string of three letters—there will be no ambiguity). The process of inventing such a symbolic system develops children's understanding of the many ways in which mathematical ideas can be communicated.

You might give children ready-made graphing formats for this activity, as shown. Children with some prior experience with graphs, however, will learn a great deal more by setting up the grids themselves. They will have to draw lines that are parallel and equally spaced and make sure there is enough room for all of the anticipated responses. Making graphs enables children to compare others' choices with their own. Lead children to use their results to determine which was the most frequently chosen color, size, and gender.

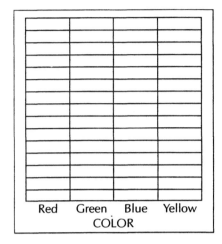

Red Green Blue Yellow
COLOR

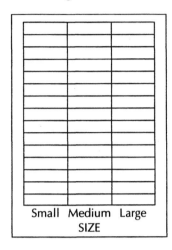

Small Medium Large
SIZE

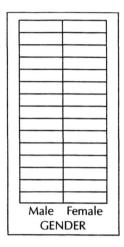

Male Female
GENDER

If several children do this activity, it would be preferable for each child to poll a different group of 20 people. Children might then compare their graphs and see if there are any general trends. Or they could combine their data into one large graph.

You can extend the activity by asking children to record something about the person they are questioning, for example, his or her age or gender. Then children can ask whether adults and children seem to differ in which size they choose to keep and whether males and females choose different types of People. Results can be displayed on double bar graphs.

HANDFULS PAGE 71

Materials: Connecting People, at least 20 pieces; a bowl or box for the pieces

Children estimate how many Connecting People there are in a handful.

Encourage children to talk about strategies they used to get better estimates. One is to take smaller handfuls. Help children to see that it makes a difference in their estimates if they pick mostly small People or mostly large People. The second part is useful for developing a good intuitive sense of 10. Children will realize that getting exactly 10 is quite difficult. They might compare their results with those of their classmates and discuss their strategies.

REACH INTO THE BAG PAGE 72

Materials: Connecting People, two 24-piece attribute sets; a paper plate or other shallow container; a paper bag

Children select a piece from one attribute set and reach into a bag containing another complete set to try and select an identical piece. They get a point for each attribute the two pieces have in common. Children keep a record of their points and the ways the two People are the same using a recording sheet like the following, which helps them to organize the record-keeping.

try	points	Check what is the same.		
		color	size	gender
1	2		✓	✓
2	3	✓	✓	✓
3	1			
4				
5				
6				
7				
8				
9				

Finally, children consider which attributes they guessed correctly most often.

Children can play this game by taking a piece quickly and randomly from the bag. They may soon realize that it is to their advantage to try and get the right person by feeling around in the bag. Therefore, they might want to agree on a time limit. Because color cannot be felt with the fingertips and because there are four possibilities, children might expect to get the color right only about one quarter of the time. They *can,* however, easily feel if a person has a skirt, so they might expect to get gender correct most of the time. (Even if the selection was completely random, children should get the right gender about half of the time.) The small People feel different from the two larger sizes; medium and large People feel more alike. If children have a choice about which person to match, they will probably do better if they try to match a small person. If they select randomly, they should get the right size about one third of the time.

Encourage children to combine the data they collected during the game and see if the patterns they notice hold for a large number of trials. You might also suggest they graph their results.

STANDING UP   PAGE 73

Materials: A small number of Connecting People

Children see which People are easier for them to stand on a table. When children play with the Connecting People they will realize that careful handling is required if the People are to remain standing.

This activity provides an interesting situation in which children can consider how to design an experiment and how to express their results, both verbally and graphically. Encourage children to form hypotheses as they work. They may sug-

Math With Connecting People™
© Learning Resources, Inc.

gest that small People fall more easily than large or that color makes no difference and gender not very much. Children will probably expect that time is a factor—People are harder to stand up if children are in a rush.

Children will need to consider how to set up an experiment to test their hypotheses. One way to design such an experiment would be to sort all the People by size and see how many of each type children could make stand in one minute. People could also be sorted by color. Many questions arise as children experiment: Does the order in which they try the types of People make a difference? Do they simply get better at setting up People with practice? Do they lose patience as they go along? Should children count People who were standing at first but then fall over? Is it helpful to set up People with sufficient space between them so that if one falls over, it doesn't knock down a neighbor? Can more People stand up on a solid table or a rickety one? Are People holding hands more likely to stay up than People standing individually? Considering these questions makes children aware of the many unexpected variables that can affect an experiment.

Children may need help in setting up a system for recording which People fall over. You might also have them consider how many times they should repeat the experiment and suggest that they ask other children to repeat their experiments to see if they get the same results.

PEOPLE COMBINATIONS   PAGE 74

Materials: Connecting People, at least two 24-piece attribute sets

Children make pairs of People and count how many different combinations they can make of color, size, or gender. This activity provides children with a context for making an organized list, and for noting patterns.

Children may need help to clarify the questions. Have them focus on different combinations by working through the first question with them. If children work with a large set of Connecting People that contains at least two of each person, there will be more possibilities for each question. Children may find that they cannot actually set up all of the possibilities because they run out of People. So they will need to invent some way of recording the pairs.

In answering the first question, children will find only three possibilities (male-male, male-female, and female-female). The second question has ten possibilities (red-red, red-green, red-blue, red-yellow, green-green, green-blue, green-yellow, blue-blue, blue-yellow, yellow-yellow). There are six possibilities for the third question (small-small, small-medium, small-large, medium-medium, medium-large, and large-large). In the fourth question, children might realize that this is just a matter of finding all possible pairs of four colors, as they did for the second question. Encourage children to ask other questions like these and to see if they can answer them without counting by recognizing the similarity to one of the questions they have already answered. As an extension, you can ask similar questions about three People who are going for a walk.

CHOOSING PEOPLE

1. If you could have just one Connecting People piece to keep, which would you choose?
   Ask 20 other people this question. Write their answers.

2. Show your results by making graphs about color, size, and gender.

Did any people agree with your choice?
Did some people agree in some way?
What was the most popular piece?

Use your graph to write about these questions.

HANDFULS

You will need more Connecting People than you can pick up in one hand.

1. Take a handful of People. Estimate how many you took. Don't count.
   Write your estimate. Then count. Write that number. Put the People back.
   Do this 10 times.
   Do your estimates keep getting closer to your counted numbers?

2. Try to pick up exactly 10 People without counting them. Then count.
   Write that number. Put the People back.
   Do this 10 times.

Did you get better at picking up exactly 10? If so, tell why.

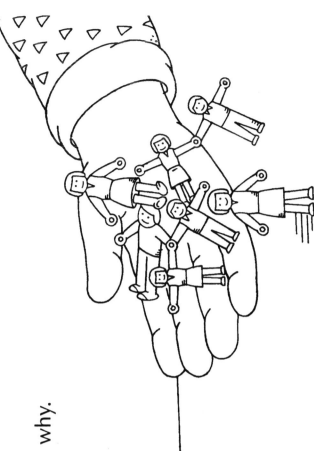

REACH INTO THE BAG

This is a game for 2 to 4 players. Take turns.

1. Choose one Connecting People piece from a plate. Reach into a bag without looking and try to choose a piece that is the same.

You get 1 point for each way they are alike—size, color, or gender.

For example, suppose you took the small red female from the plate. This is how many points you would get if you picked these People from the bag...

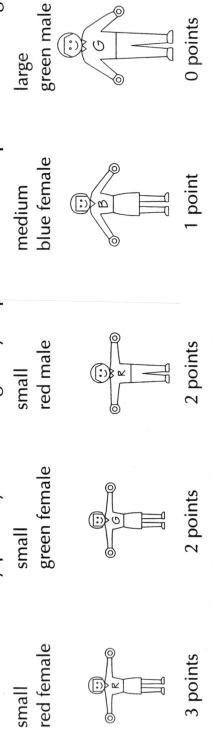

small red female	small green female	small red male	medium blue female	large green male
3 points	2 points	2 points	1 point	0 points

Keep a record of the ways the People are the same.

2. Do this 10 times.

3. Add your scores. The winner is the player with the most points. Use your record to write about these questions. What were you right about most often? Was it size, color, or gender? Can you tell why?

Math With Connecting People™
© Learning Resources, Inc.

STANDING UP

Work with a partner.

Connecting People sometimes fall over when you try to make them stand.

1. Stand some People on the table. Is it easier to make some People stand than others?

2. How can you find out which People are easiest to make stand?
   Design an experiment to see.

Compare your results with some of your classmates' results.
Tell one another exactly what you did.
Does what you did make a difference?

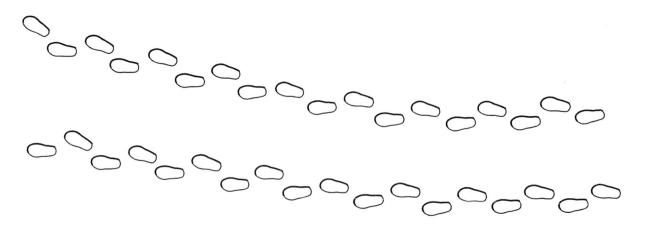

PEOPLE COMBINATIONS

Two Connecting People are going for a walk. Their hands are joined.

How many combinations of two People can there be if...

• both are small red People?
• both are small females?
• both are red females?
• both are large males?

How can you show your combinations?

Are the answers to any of these questions the same? If so, tell why.

ADDITIONAL RESOURCES

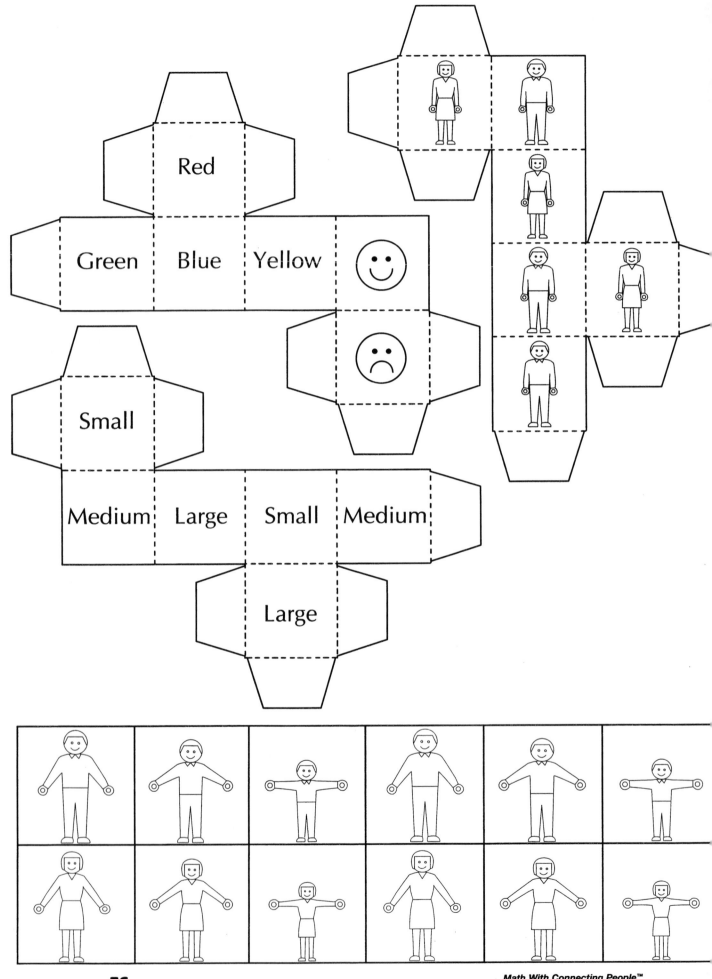

small	medium	large
not small	not medium	not large
red	blue	green
not red	not blue	not green
yellow	male	female
not yellow	not male	not female

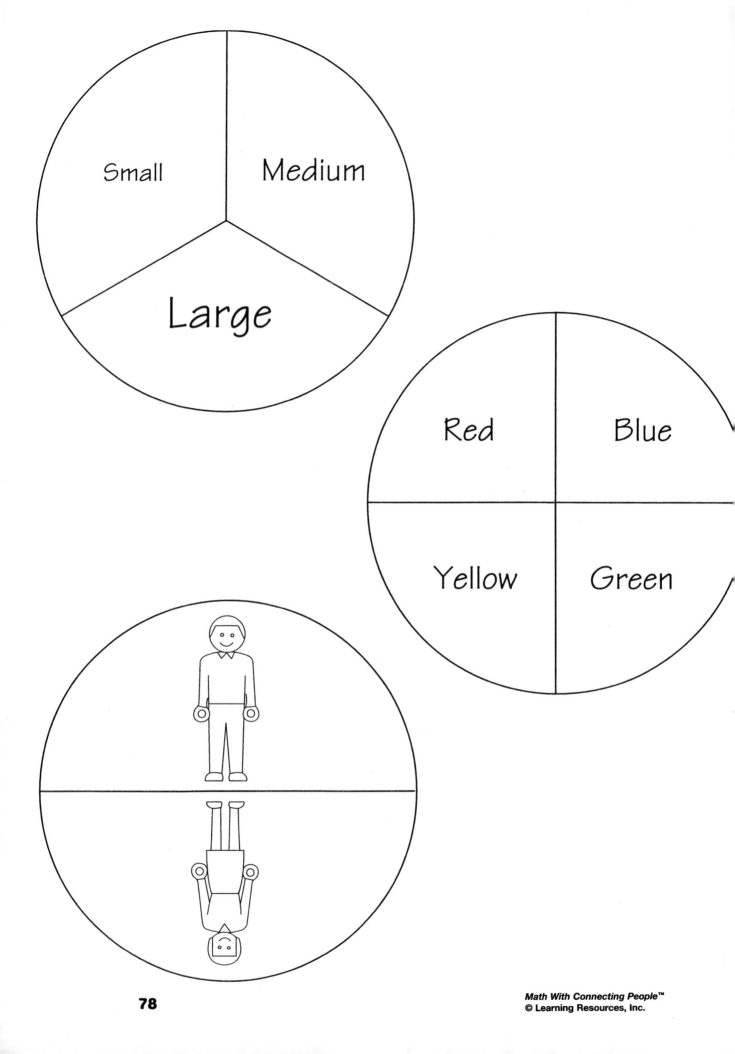

	79

Male   Female

GENDER

Small   Medium   Large

SIZE

Red   Green   Blue   Yellow

COLOR